The Alpaca and Alfalfa Alphabet Book

Dr. Gerald Young

ISBN: 978-1-897478-07-3
Published by Dr. Gerald Young
Rejoining Joy Publishing Inc.
Toronto, Ontario Canada

Cover and text design: WeMakeBooks.ca
Printed in Canada

Preface

To see the full range of the works by Dr. Young on rejoining joy,
consult the website www.rejoiningjoy.com. The primary theme in the work of Gerald Young
relates to rejoining joy. Joy is not a given, but is a lived moment that is earned and requires sharing,
working through, and responsibility. With the right attitude, we can rejoin joy in all our human
activities and, as we deal with stress, illness, or injury, we can rejoin it by our hope and mindful
planning and follow through. The skill of rejoining joy can be learned and can become a way of life
no matter what our age or circumstance. The present work teaches and inspires toward that end,
showing how to promote positives and control negatives, whether in terms of our inner feelings,
dealing with others, including our partners and family, and getting through
the activities of the day.

Dedicated to
all the animals and children.

Alligators, aardvarks — an alphabet of animals. From armored armadillos to acrobatic ants, they prance and dance.

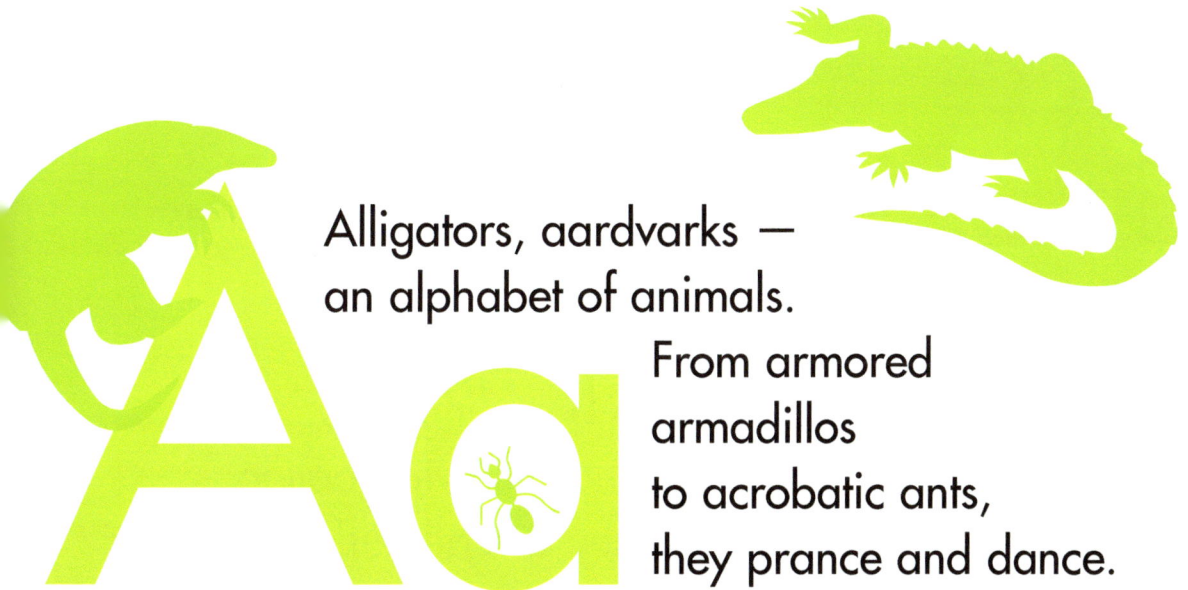

Alligators, aardvarks —
an alphabet of animals.
From armored
armadillos
to acrobatic ants,
they prance and dance.

Baby bears, to bouncing beetles and babbling baboons; bantering birds, to barreling bats and billowing balloons —they are all buffoons.

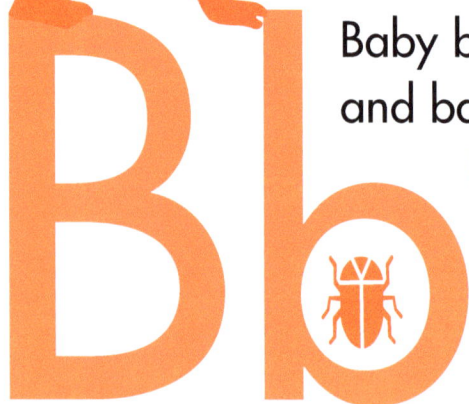

Baby bears, to bouncing beetles
and babbling baboons;
bantering birds,
to barreling bats
and billowing balloons —
they are all buffoons.

Coyotes chase a caribou, cheetahs a chimpanzee. But the camouflaged chameleon is carefree. Cute cats and cuddly kittens chant in chorus with children and chickens.

Cute cats and cuddly kittens chant in chorus with children and chickens. Coyotes chase a caribou, cheetahs a chimpanzee. But the camouflaged chameleon is carefree.

Deer and dogs dance in the light. But dragons dream in the dark of the night.

Ducks and dolphins swim with delight.

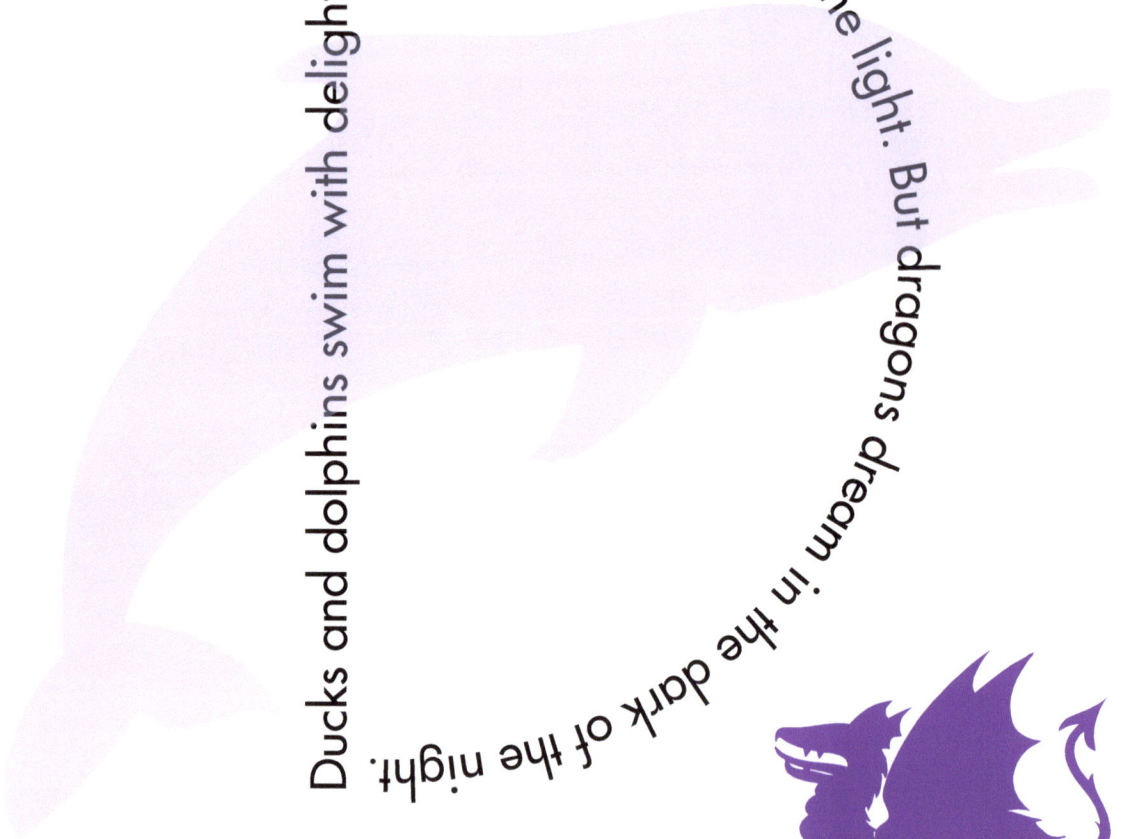

Dd

Ducks and dolphins
swim with delight.
Deer and dogs
dance in the light.
But dragons dream
in the dark of the night.

eels electrify energetically,

When eagles elevate elegantly and

elephants eat enormously

and elks enjoy endlessly.

E e

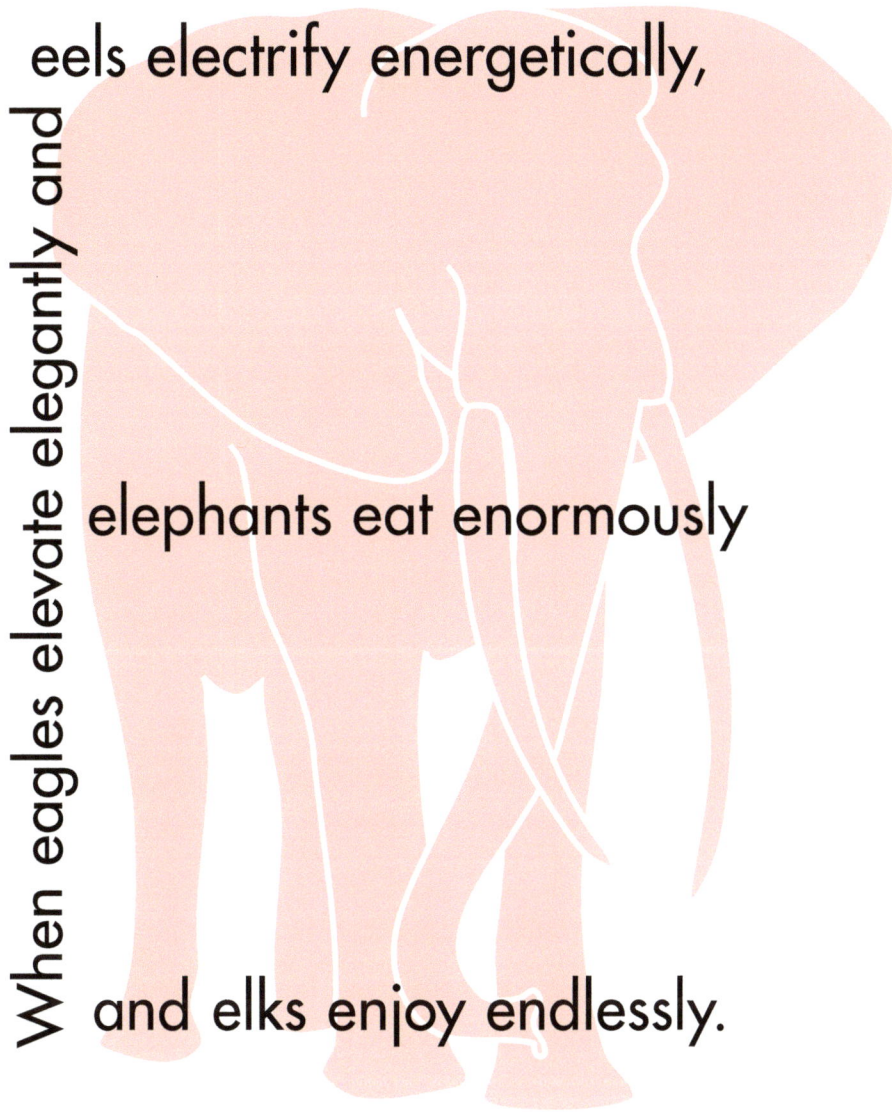

When eagles elevate elegantly
and eels electrify energetically,
elephants eat enormously
and elks enjoy endlessly.

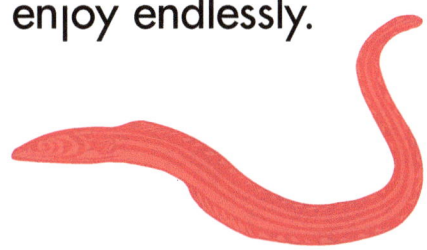

Falcons fly, foxes find, fish flee, fireflies flame, flamingoes have fun, and frogs frolic.

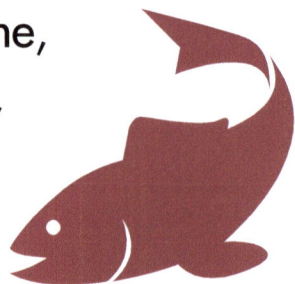

Ff

Falcons fly, foxes find, fish flee, fireflies flame, flamingoes have fun, and frogs frolic.

Gazelles gambol, geckos gyrate, giraffes elongate, goats graze, geese gather, and gorillas grow.

Gazelles gambol,

Gg

Gazelles gambol,
geckos gyrate,
giraffes elongate,
goats graze,
geese gather,
and
gorillas grow.

Hawks, herons, and hummingbirds are sky high. Hornets and honeybees also fly. But hares, hedgehogs, hippopotami, horses, and hyenas all ask how and why.

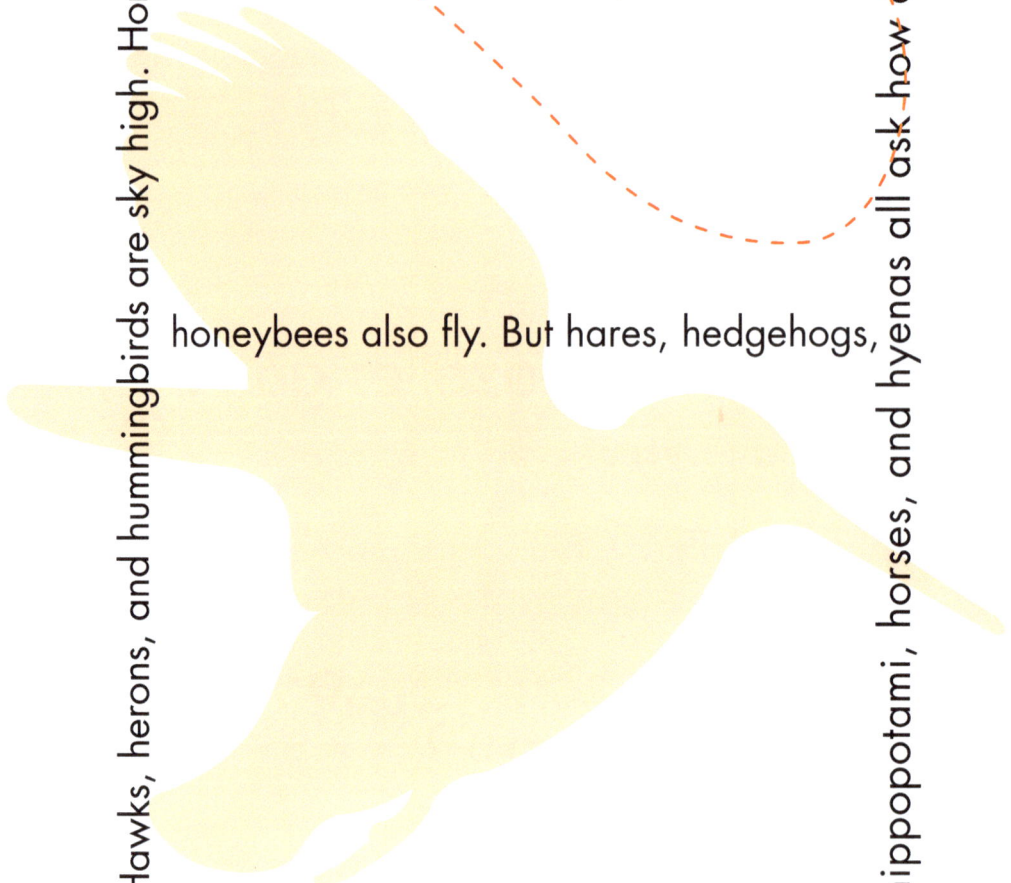

Hh

Hawks, herons, and hummingbirds are sky high. Hornets and honeybees also fly. But hares, hedgehogs, hippopotami, horses, and hyenas all ask how and why.

If an ibis likes an ibex, does an iguana like an impala?

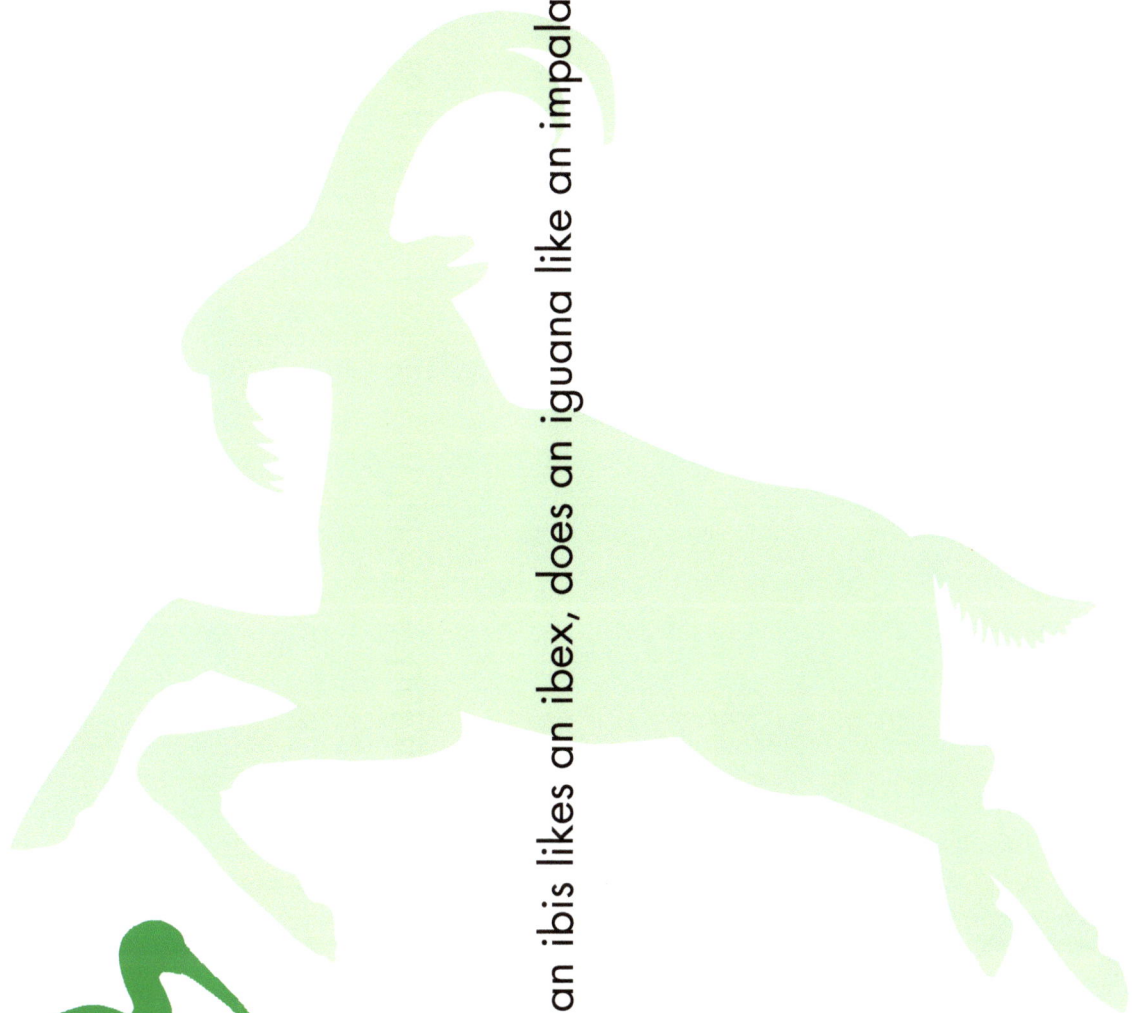

Ii

If an ibis
likes an ibex,
does an iguana
like an impala?

Joeys jump at jaguars in jungles, but not at jays joyriding jellyfish.

Jj

Joeys jump at
jaguars in jungles,
but not at
jays joyriding
jellyfish.

Kung Fu kiddies kiss kangaroos and koalas, kingfishers and kiwi, and kinkajous and kookaburras.

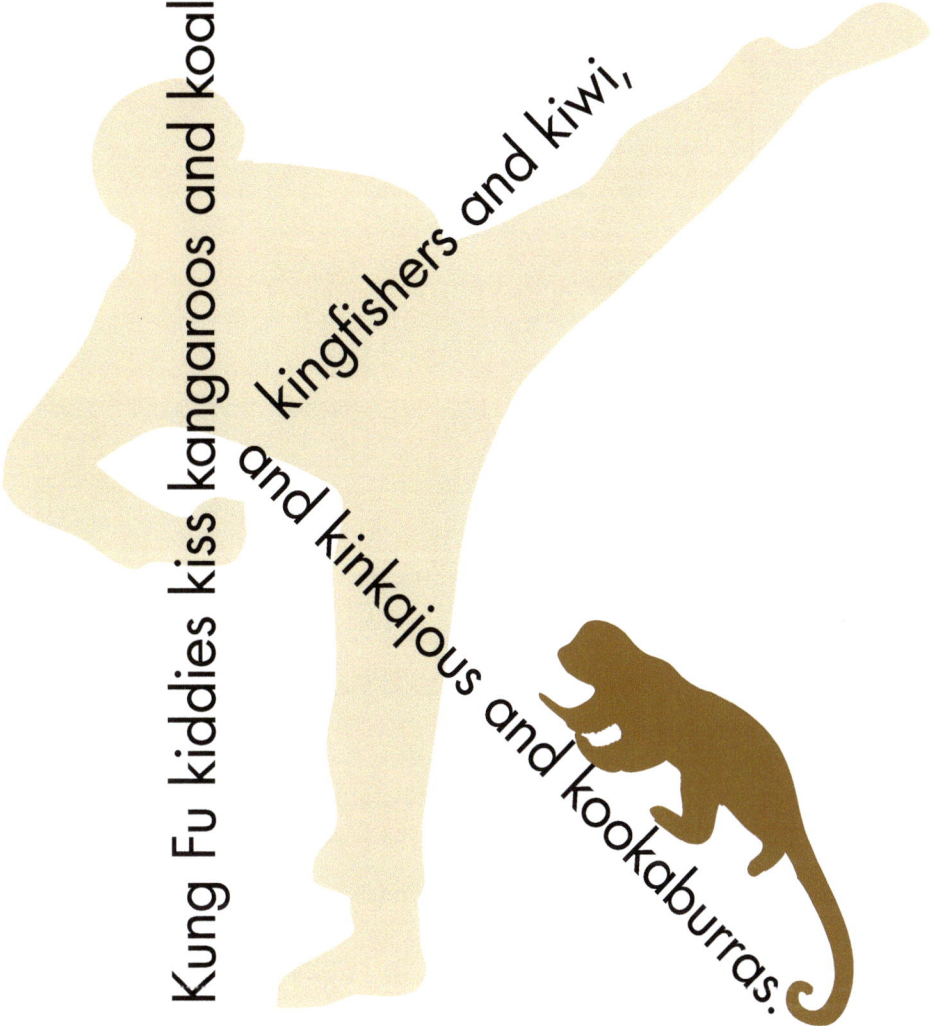

Kk

Kung Fu
kiddies kiss
kangaroos and koalas,
kingfishers and kiwi,
and kinkajous
and kookaburras.

Lions, leopards, and lynx laugh with

llamas, lemurs, and langurs.

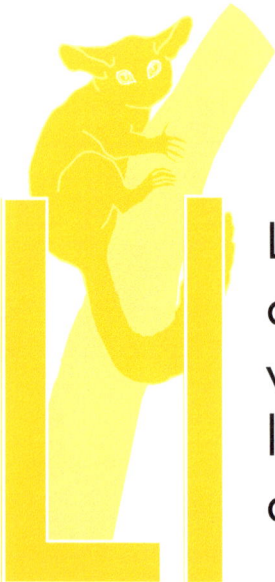

Ll

Lions, leopards, and lynx laugh with llamas, lemurs, and langurs.

Mice and moles like to play; mandrils and meerkats, too. But monarchs and macaws riding moose are the merriest in the zoo.

Mm

Mice and moles like to play;
mandrils and meerkats, too.
But monarchs and macaws
riding moose
are the merriest
in the zoo.

The nightingale alighted on the narwal's tusk. They chirped and sang until the dusk. Then their noses smelled the musk.

Nn

The nightingale alighted
on the narwal's tusk.
They chirped and sang
until the dusk.
Then their noses
smelled the musk.

Otters go circles around opossum, ostriches around orangutans, octopuses around oysters, and owls around orioles.

Otters go circles around opossum, ostriches around orangutans, octopuses around oysters, and owls around orioles.

Parrots, peacocks, pelicans, and penguins have wings. But pandas and porcupines sing and sting.

Pp

Parrots, peacocks, pelicans, and penguins have wings. But pandas and porcupines sing and sting.

When queen ants and quarrel, quails and quetzels quit, quack, and quiver When queen ants and queen bees quake

When queen ants
and queen bees
quake and quarrel,
quails and quetzels
quit, quack, and quiver.

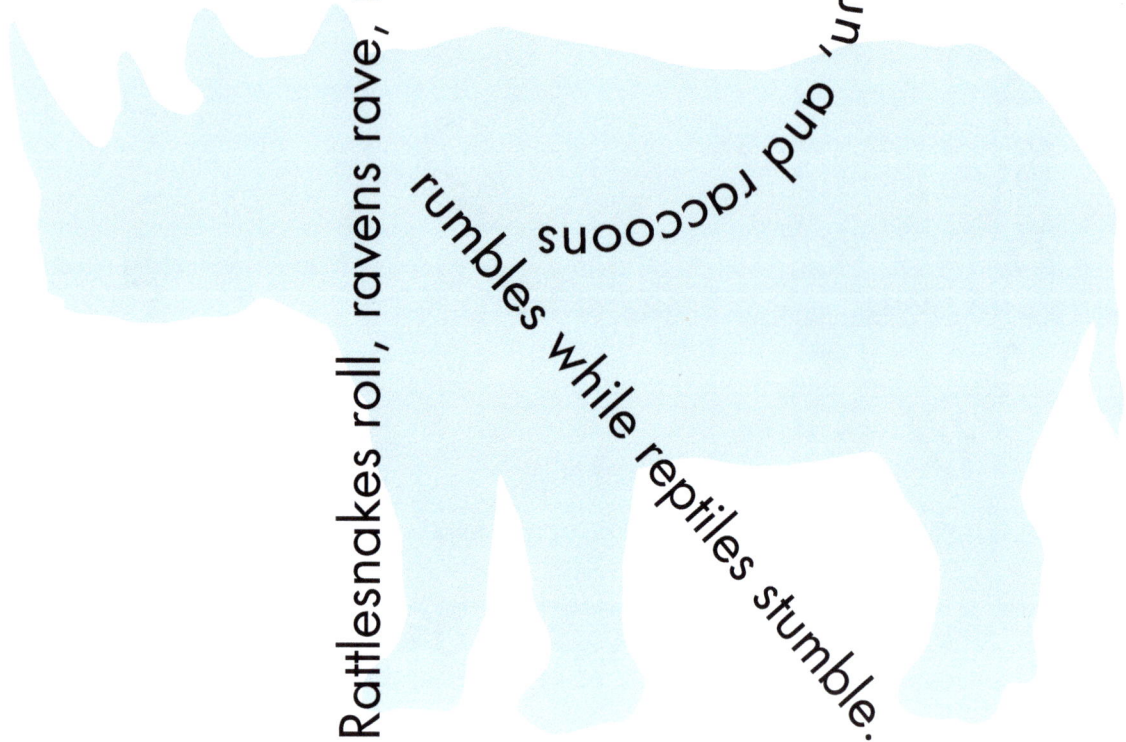

Rattlesnakes roll, ravens rave, rhinoceroses stroll, rats race, rabbits run, and raccoons rumbles while reptiles stumble.

Rr

Rattlesnakes roll, ravens rave, rhinoceroses stroll, rats race, rabbits run, and raccoons rumble, while reptiles stumble.

To see salmon, seahorses, starfish, stingrays, seals, and sharks, scoot to the sea. When sheep, squirrels, salamanders, scorpions, and storks see a skunk, they flee.

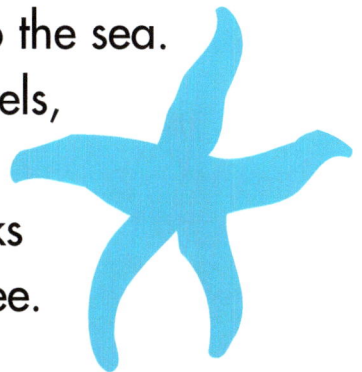

To see salmon, seahorses,
starfish, stingrays, seals,
and sharks, scoot to the sea.
When sheep, squirrels,
salamanders,
scorpions, and storks
see a skunk, they flee.

Turtles, toads, tunas, and turkeys tease

tarantulas, tigers, and tyrannosauruses.

T t

Turtles, toads, tunas, and turkeys tease
tarantulas, tigers, and tyrannosauruses.

Uakaris under trees and ungulates under stars unite with unicorns under umbrellas.

Uakaris under trees and ungulates under stars unite with unicorns under umbrellas.

Vultures view vicunas and vervets, and vipers view voles on velvet.

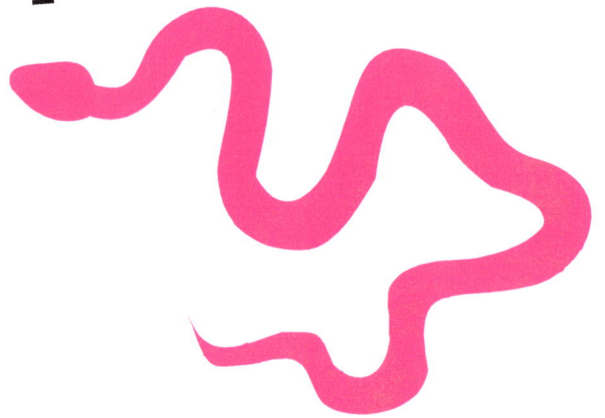

Vv

Vultures view vicunas and vervets, and vipers view voles on velvet.

Whales and walruses swim in water; warblers and wrens fly in wind; while wolves and wildebeest walk on ways.

Whales and walruses
swim in water;
warblers and wrens
fly in wind; while
wolves and wildebeest
walk on ways.

Ww

Zoos are for animals to help them thrive.
From Xenosaurs and oXen, to Yaks and Zebras
we can all help animals survive.

XYZ

www.ingramcontent.com/pod-product-compliance
Lightning Source LLC
Chambersburg PA
CBHW060855270326
41934CB00002B/147